Contents

Wi, t is a portr it?

A portrait is a picture or photograph of a person. These children had to stand very still to have their portraits painted.

The Children of Charles I by Catherine Read (18th century)

Let's look at
Children

Barbara Hunter

Heinemann
LIBRARY

www.heinemann.co.uk/library
Visit our website to find out more information about **Heinemann Library** books.

To order:
 Phone 44 (0) 1865 888066
Send a fax to 44 (0) 1865 314091
Visit the Heinemann Bookshop at www.heinemann.co.uk/library to browse our catalogue and order online.

First published in Great Britain by Heinemann Library, Halley Court, Jordan Hill, Oxford OX2 8EJ, part of Harcourt Education.
Heinemann is a registered trademark of Harcourt Education Ltd.

Editorial: Jilly Attwood and Claire Throp
Design: Jo Hinton-Malivoire and bigtop, Bicester, UK
Models made by: Jo Brooker
Picture Research: Catherine Bevan
Production: Lorraine Warner

Originated by Dot Gradations
Printed and bound in China by South China Printing Company

ISBN 0 431 16381 2 (hardback)
06 05 04 03 02
10 9 8 7 6 5 4 3 2 1

ISBN 0 431 16386 3 (paperback)
06 05 04 03 02
10 9 8 7 6 5 4 3 2 1

British Library Cataloguing in Publication Data
Hunter, Barbara
Let's Look at Children
704.9'425
A full catalogue record for this book is available from the British Library.

Acknowledgements
The publishers would like to thank the following for permission to reproduce photographs:
Art Institute of Chicago, © 2002 p. **14**; Bolton Museum and Art Gallery, Lancashire, UK/Bridgeman Art Library p. **4**; Bridgeman Art Library p. **11**; Butler Institute of American Art, Youngstown OH, USA/Bridgeman Art Library p. **10**; Kunstmuseum Bern pp. **20/21**; Musee d'Orsay, Paris, France/Giraudon/Bridgeman Art Library p. **23**; National Gallery, London, UK/Bridgeman Art Library p. **9**; Private Collection, Bonhams, London, UK/Bridgeman Art Library p. **19**; Private Collection/Bridgeman Art Library pp. **15, 16/17**; RMN/J. G. Berizzi p. **22**; Siobhan Cummings p. **7**; The Art Archive/I.U.F.M. Paris / Dagli Orti p. **18**;The Drambuie Collection, Edinburgh, Scotland/Bridgeman Art Library p. **12**;The White Pierrot, 1901/1902 by Pierre Auguste Renoir, Bequest of Robert H. Tannahill, Photograph: The Detroit Institute of Arts, © 1986 p. **13**.

Cover photograph reproduced with permission of Bridgeman Art Library/private collection

The publishers would like to thank Annie Davy for her assistance in the preparation of this book.

Every effort has been made to contact copyright holders of any material reproduced in this book. Any omissions will be rectified in subsequent printings if notice is given to the publishers.

It only takes a few seconds
to take a photograph. It takes
much longer to paint a picture.

Self-portraits

This is a photograph of Siobhan when she was four years old.

This is a self-portrait of Siobhan
when she was four years old.

Why isn't this girl playing with her hoop and stick?

Look at her face. How do you think she feels about not playing with them?

The Umbrellas by Pierre Auguste Renoir (c. 1881–86)

Games

These boys are playing a running game. How can you tell they are running?

Snap the Whip by Winslow Homer (1872)
Children's Games by Pieter Bruegel the Elder (1560)

Can you see all the different games these children are playing?

Dressing up

Is this picture light or dark?

Little Soldier by John Burr (19th century)

Does this boy look like he is having fun?

The White Pierrot by Pierre Auguste Renoir (1905)

Dancing

This painting is called 'Dancing Girl'.
How do you know she is dancing?

Dancing Girl by Paul Klee

This is a sculpture of a ballet dancer. This model is made from metal.

Little Dancer, aged 14 by Edgar Degas (c. 1920–21)

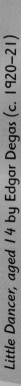

15

Cooking

What can you *see* in this picture? Can you find the boy licking the spoon?

Christmas Pudding by Gillian Lawson (20th century)

At school

These children are at school. Does it look the same as your school?

Nursery School by Jan Jules Geoffrey (1898)

Kept In by John Henry Henshall (1905)

These two children have been kept in school. Do they look happy?

Stories

This boy is reading to his grandfather.

Can you see the marks made by the artist's brush?

Die Andacht des Grossvaters by Albert Anker (1893)

Sleeping

Can you see the pencil lines in this drawing?

Portrait of Juliette Courbet asleep on her book by Gustave Courbet (1841)

Can you see the sleeping baby?

The Cradle by Berthe Morisot (1872)

Index

The end

Notes for adults

This series covers the creative development area of learning. Each book looks at works of art from different cultures and different media. This set of books will support the young child's learning about the world around them and provide opportunities for them to explore different types of art. The following key Early Learning Goals are relevant to this series:
• explore colour, texture, shape, form and space in two or three dimensions
• respond in a variety of ways to what they see, hear, smell, touch and feel
• use their imagination in art and design.

Lets Look at Children includes pictures of children shown doing everyday things, such as playing and sleeping. It also has old paintings showing games and toys children may have played with in the past, that children today may never have seen or heard of.

Children will need to explore the differences between a 2-D painting and a 3-D sculpture and it will be necessary to explain that some artists represent their work in a literal way, like a photograph, while some paint or draw how an object 'feels' to them so it may not look like the 'real thing'. Discussing how some objects make children feel, or what they are reminded of when they see them, can help understanding.

Key vocabulary that can be explored through this book includes *portrait, photograph, shadow, dark, sculpture, metal* and *pencil lines*.

Follow-up activities
Children could make a diary of all the things they would do in an average day/week e.g. Tuesday: Dancing. The children could then show what they did on each day by painting, drawing or taking a photograph.

Self-portraits using different media could be another follow-up activity. They could try painting their portrait with thick or thin paints, drawing with lead or coloured pencils and making a sculpture of their face using clay, plasticene or paper.